EXTREME CAREERS

SECRET AGENTS
Life as a Professional Spy

Claudia B. Manley

the rosen publishing group's
rosen central

Published in 2001 by The Rosen Publishing Group, Inc.
29 East 21st Street, New York, NY 10010

Copyright © 2001 by The Rosen Publishing Group, Inc.

First Edition

Library of Congress Cataloging-in-Publication Data

Manley, Claudia B.
Secret agents: life as a professional spy / by Claudia B. Manley.—
1st ed.
p. cm. — (Extreme careers)
Includes bibliographical references and index.
ISBN 0-8239-3369-5
1. Spies—Juvenile literature. 2. Espionage—Vocational guidance—
Juvenile literature. [1. Spies. 2. Espionage—Vocational guidance.
3. Vocational guidance.] I. Title. II. Series.
UB270.5 .M36 2001
327.12'023—dc21
                                                        00-012714

Manufactured in the United States of America

Contents

Top Secret

Alex tucks the pen camera inside the breast pocket of his tuxedo and scales the walls of the foreign defense minister's mansion. Inside, at the crowded party, his partner, Leonora, sips champagne. She is prepared to create a diversion at exactly 11:45 PM. Alex glances at his watch. He has only five minutes to get to the safe in the minister's bedroom.

He continues toward the bedroom window. It's now 11:43 PM! Time is running out. There is a nuclear warhead pointed at Washington, DC, and this is the only chance to defuse it. Alex must find the secret codes inside the safe before the United States is blown to bits.

He pries open the window and slips inside.
From downstairs comes a loud crash, followed
by a lot of commotion. Leonora has done her
job! Just as he reaches the safe, he hears the
door open behind him . . .

Have you ever listened in on your brother's phone conversations to his girlfriend? Or pretended you were saving the world from an evil villain, who also happened to be your grumpy next-door neighbor? Chances are, at one time or another, you've dreamt of being a spy. And who hasn't? In the movies and on television, spies, or secret agents, are always portrayed as smooth-talking, adventurous people who live glamorous lives.

Spies are not just fictional characters. They have been around for as long as people and societies have fought against their enemies. Ancient Greek leaders relied on spies to help them win battles. *The Art of War*, written in China all the way back in 400 BC, but still used today as a guidebook for military commanders and strategists, stressed the need for secrecy and spying to beat the enemy. It is even

Nathan Hale, one of the earliest secret agents in the history of the United States, was hanged by the British in 1776.

believed that Moses sent agents to spy on the people of Canaan so that the Israelites would be able to return to the land and conquer it.

For a government to prosper, it helps to have certain information about the world around it. However, this information, often called intelligence, is not always easily available. The right intelligence helps influence national decisions. Incorrect information, or information that gets into the wrong hands, can result in disaster for both the agents who obtain it and the government they're working for.

One of the earliest agents in the history of the United States was a Revolutionary War spy named Nathan Hale (1755–1776). Hale joined the U.S. Army in 1775 and became a captain a year later. When he came to New York in 1776, he volunteered for an assignment to spy on British troops stationed on Long Island.

Because Hale was well educated, he went undercover as a Dutch schoolmaster. He collected as much information about the enemy as he could, but when he tried to return to his regiment to give them his report, he was caught by the British and sentenced to die. When asked for his last words, he said, "I only regret that I have but one life to lose for my country." Nathan Hale was hanged on September 22, 1776.

Secret Agents: Life as a Professional Spy

Like Nathan Hale, many agents are motivated by a commitment to their country and a willingness to make the ultimate sacrifice—their lives—for it.

You can already see that being a secret agent is not all glamour. There's some real danger involved. After reading this book, you may decide that it's more than you bargained for. Or you might find that it's the perfect career for you!

Secret Agents in Pop Culture

Most of our ideas about secret agents have come from popular culture—from books, TV shows, and movies. Very few of us know real-life spies. They don't exactly advertise themselves as such. Secrecy is the very nature of their profession. Chances are, if your next-door neighbor were a secret agent, he or she would pose as someone more ordinary, like a professor or office worker, in order to keep a low profile and be an effective spy.

Books

The Library of Congress contains records for thousands of books about spies and secret agents. It seems that

Pierce Brosnan stars as the ultrasmooth James Bond, the best-known fictional secret agent, in the movie *GoldenEye*.

people never tire of reading a good tale of espionage. Aside from giving us a gripping story, these books can provide great insight into the political climate of a certain time and place.

Everybody knows who James Bond is. He is probably the best-known secret agent, and the model for many others. As the ultrasmooth 007, millions of people have followed him as he has battled threats to the security of Great Britain and the entire world. Along the way, there have been plenty of obstacles, and women, who try to get in the way of his success.

The writer Ian Fleming created the character of James Bond in 1957. Since Fleming's death, different authors have taken over the writing. New James Bond novels are still being written today! Of course, most of us are fans of the Bond movie franchise, which has continued for more than forty years.

There have been countless other books that feature secret agents as their subjects. John LeCarré, Tom Clancy, and Nelson DeMille are just a few popular espionage writers of today.

Television

In response to the Cold War (1947–1991), American and British television aired many spy-related television shows. Tensions between Western and Communist nations—especially between the United States and the Soviet Union—were high. Neither country trusted the other, and both aimed for world dominance. Shows like *The Man from U.N.C.L.E.*, *I Spy*, and *Get Smart* featured secret agents, both

I Spy was one of many popular television shows inspired by the work of secret agents during the Cold War.

comical and serious, saving the world from deadly bombs and assassination attempts. These shows comforted the often frightened American public by making them believe that agents were working hard to protect them from threatening forces.

In the '80s, television brought us spy shows like *The Scarecrow and Mrs. King* and *MacGyver*. When the Cold War came to a close, the shows no longer pitted the American or British agent against an evil Eastern European villain. As the U.S. intelligence community (IC) shifted its focus, television and popular culture followed suit. These days, television shows that focus on the adventures of secret agents are not as common, but they are still fascinating to viewers.

Movies

Current versions of the spy myth are mostly on film, and many of these films are based on television

In a scene from the big-screen version of *Mission: Impossible*, Tom Cruise hangs from the ceiling as he taps into a computer to steal enemy information.

series from the 1960s and 1970s. *Mission: Impossible* was originally a television show that aired from 1966 to 1973. Every week the team of agents had a mission that they could choose to accept or not. Of course they always accepted, and the result was sixty minutes of tension and excitement. In recent years, *MI* has made it to the big screen and features an agent who, while still smooth and elegant, is a little more contemporary: He rides a motorcycle and dangles from cliffs for fun.

Based on the British series of the same name, the 1998 film *The Avengers* paired the stylish and brilliant secret agent Emma Peel with quintessentially British James Steed. As a crime-fighting duo, they flirted with danger and with each other.

Not all spy movies are based on successful TV series from the '60s and '70s. Some are realistic thrillers. *The Falcon and the Snowman* dramatized the real-life story of two former altar boys who sold secrets to the Soviets in the 1970s. Hollywood has even found humor in espionage. *Spies Like Us* and the Austin Powers movies spoof a very serious business.

Mata Hari

All well-known spies are not necessarily fictitious. Some real-life secret agents have seeped into our popular culture as well. Margaretha Geertruida Zelle, also known as Mata Hari, symbolizes the glamorous secret agent who seduces her enemies to get even the best-kept secrets. While Mata Hari may have been an accomplished seductress, she was not an accomplished spy.

Posing as an Indonesian dancer in Paris, the Dutch beauty gained fame throughout

Mata Hari used her glamour as an exotic dancer to seduce enemies of Germany into revealing even the best-kept secrets.

Profile: Julius and Ethel Rosenberg

Spies or victims? The world will never know.

Julius Rosenberg and his wife, Ethel, were the first American civilians to be executed for treason, or disloyalty to their country, during peacetime. Convicted in 1951 of giving atomic military secrets to Russia, they became symbols of all that frightened Americans during that time in history.

The atomic bomb was the deadliest weapon in the world, and the United States was the only country that knew how to make one. When Russia revealed proof that they, too, had atomic bomb capabilities, America panicked. Communism was spreading throughout the world and America's security was at stake. Because they were members of the Communist Party, the Rosenbergs were seen as an automatic threat. After two years of unsuccessful court appeals, they

were electrocuted on June 19, 1953. Since then, many people have concluded that the Rosenbergs were treated unfairly and convicted on flimsy evidence.

Europe in the early 1900s. She was also known to have quite a few lovers, many of whom were military officers in World War I.

When her dancing career ended, she tried working for both the French and the German governments. Her relationships with high-ranking officers gave her access to a lot of classified information, which she tried to use for money and privileges. One account of Mata Hari's career states that a German diplomat in the Netherlands offered her money for top-secret information about France. When the French government found out that Mata Hari had been working not only for them, but for the Germans as well, they accused her of treason. She was arrested in Paris and imprisoned, tried, and shot by a firing squad on October 15, 1917.

Mata Hari's espionage may have been more accidental than intentional. There is a lot of evidence to support the theory that she really didn't understand the consequences of her actions. Her story teaches us that spying is not a game to be taken lightly.

Throughout the twentieth century, women continued to be used as spies by governments and organizations. Often, they would lure top political leaders into compromising situations, then use bribery to get secrets they could pass on to enemy governments.

Who Wants You?

If you decide that you want to be a spy, there are plenty of organizations in the United States and throughout the world that might need your help.

The United States Intelligence Community

In the United States, most secret agents belong to what is known as the intelligence community. The IC is made up of different government agencies that need the services of secret agents. The agencies include the CIA and the FBI, as well as each branch of the armed services and agencies like the Department of Transportation and the Department of Energy.

DCI

Each of the intelligence community agencies is overseen by the Director of Central Intelligence (DCI). Every year, the DCI puts together the budget for the intelligence agencies and presents it to Congress. The DCI has to determine the intelligence needs of the country and how the necessary information will be retrieved, as well as what steps agencies have to take to protect their own information. All of these steps cost money, and the DCI needs to make sure that there is enough for each agency.

CIA

The Central Intelligence Agency is the best-known employer of agents. Created by President Harry Truman in 1947, the CIA is responsible for getting

CIA agents spend a lot of time and energy collecting information and writing reports that explain all the information they find.

information about other countries, and also for counterintelligence, or safeguarding secrets about our own country.

When the plans and goals of U.S. foreign policy can't be achieved by talking and cooperating with other nations, but using military force would be too extreme, the National Security Council (NSC) recommends a covert, or secret, activity. With covert activities, the role of the U.S. government is not advertised or publicly known.

The CIA spends a lot of time and energy collecting and interpreting information. That's why it hires all different types of people with various specialties, like scientists, engineers, accountants, and even mathematicians. Agents must be able to do research and write reports that explain all of the information they find. That doesn't sound quite as glamorous as James Bond, does it?

FBI

The Federal Bureau of Investigation serves as the investigative branch of the U.S. Department of Justice. Its priorities include counterterrorism (eliminating terrorist

U.S. Secret Service agents provide protection for President George W. Bush during the inaugural parade on January 20, 2001.

threats to the United States), foreign counterintelligence, and criminal investigation. The FBI also performs background checks on people nominated for important government positions, like the secretary of health and human services or a Supreme Court justice.

Department of Defense

Each military branch of the Department of Defense has its own intelligence division. Unlike the CIA and FBI, which have authority for a much broader scope, these branches focus primarily on military issues. Under the direction of the Defense Intelligence Agency, the army, navy, air force, and marines all have divisions that monitor the kinds of weapons and technologies other countries have. They also keep their eyes on new developments in foreign militaries and threats to the U.S. military.

Secret Service

The U.S. Secret Service's best-known job is the protection of the president, the vice president, and their families. Secret Service agents are members of

Profile: Alger Hiss

An elegant, intelligent, high-ranking federal employee, Alger Hiss was yet another person brought down by the Red Scare. Under investigation for having communist ties, Hiss revealed information that led officials to believe he was a spy.

Although all evidence used against him was less than airtight and came from an unreliable source, he was nevertheless condemned by his own government. After one trial that ended in a hung jury, he was tried again and convicted of perjury. The only thing that saved him from going to prison for being a spy was time. The three-year statute of limitations had expired and all the evidence was too old.

A lot of people benefited from Hiss's conviction and imprisonment. One was a young congressman named Richard Nixon, who used his success and the fame he gained as head of the investigation to win a senate seat and, later, the presidency.

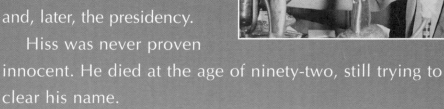

Hiss was never proven innocent. He died at the age of ninety-two, still trying to clear his name.

the U.S. Treasury Department, so they also investigate counterfeiting.

National Security Agency

The National Security Agency's main concern is signals intelligence, the making and breaking of secret codes. Agents for the NSA learn to understand foreign communications—not only the languages, but the codes used by foreign countries.

Department of State

The Department of State has a separate Bureau of Intelligence, which gathers information on countries where the United States has representatives. This bureau analyzes and interprets what's going on around the world. It looks at events, like elections or civil unrest, and figures out how they will affect the United States.

Department of Energy

The Department of Energy's intelligence efforts focus on energy, national security, science, and technology

A Mossad spy, hidden by a Swiss police officer, enters the Swiss Federal Tribunal in Lausanne, Switzerland, on June 3, 2000.

information. This branch of the intelligence community helps to keep our energy sources secure. It also provides information on new ways to use our energy and how to be more competitive in the global energy marketplace.

Spies in Other Countries

When talking about secret agents, there is a tendency to think only of superpowers, such as the United States and the former Soviet Union. But many countries of different sizes and economic structures have employed spies. Most countries have their own intelligence communities.

The two main agencies in the United Kingdom are the Secret Intelligence Service, also known as MI-6, and the Security Service, also known as MI-5. The MI-6 is like the CIA in the United States, but while the director of the CIA is a known public figure, the director of the MI-6 is referred to only as "C" and is anonymous. The MI-5 is like the FBI.

Israel has a rather extensive intelligence community made up of five different organizations. The Central

Institute for Intelligence and Security, also popularly known as Mossad, concerns itself primarily with espionage and covert political activities. The Shin Bet works with internal counterintelligence. There is also the Intelligence Corps of Defense, which is Israel's military intelligence division. The Research Department of the Foreign Ministry focuses on political information, and the Special Investigations Department of the Israel Police Force is mainly concerned with criminal activities within the borders of Israel.

Double Agents

During the period of the Cold War, the Soviet Union's KGB and the United States's CIA were constantly trying to get information about one another. The competition to outsmart the other led to a growth in the number of double agents. A double agent is someone employed as an agent by one country who is recruited by a second country to spy on the country that originally hired him or her. The job of double agent definitely requires someone who can think on his or her feet!

Members of the infamous Soviet spy ring that operated in Britain during World War II are *(clockwise from upper left)* Sir Anthony Blunt, Donald Maclean, Guy Burgess, and Kim Philby.

Secret Agents: Life as a Professional Spy

Anthony Blunt (1907–1983), Kim Philby (1912–1988), Guy Burgess (1911–1963), and Donald Maclean (1913–1983) are perhaps history's most notorious double agents. They were motivated by ideology—by a strong belief in a political philosophy. All four held high positions in the British intelligence community. What no one else knew was that their real allegiance was to the Soviet Union.

As part of the MI-6, Philby and Burgess were able to keep fellow spies from being detected. Maclean worked his way to the top of the Foreign Office, which allowed him to provide the Soviet Union with highly classified material, including information on the development of the North Atlantic Treaty Organization (NATO). Blunt served the MI-5 while working as an art adviser to Queen Elizabeth, who granted him knighthood.

In May 1951, Burgess and Maclean were warned by Philby that British and American intelligence were beginning to suspect them of espionage. Eventually, all four left British intelligence and moved to Moscow, where it was safe to be open about their communist beliefs. Blunt has the distinction of the longest active, undetected run as a spy. His admission of guilt caused the British government to strip him of his knighthood.

What's Expected of a Spy?

Being a secret agent means being able to report important information to the right people. You have to be able to do this even though other countries are trying their best to keep you from that very information.

Information: How to Get It and What to Do with It

The three main jobs of an agent are collecting, interpreting, and delivering information. This may seem simple, but achieving success as a spy requires a quick-thinking, intelligent person who can work in pressure-filled and often dangerous conditions.

Collecting

Collecting information means finding the most accurate and up-to-date sources. These could be newspapers and magazines, foreign policy reports, or local and national radio and television broadcasts. All of these sources help agents understand the way events are described locally, often as government propaganda.

In some cases, agents will travel to get intelligence firsthand. They might try to meet people who work in the government or groups that oppose the government. They will often adopt a disguise of some sort, introducing themselves as professors or other professionals who might have use for that kind of knowledge.

Interpreting

Interpreting information is even more difficult than stealing it. Some information is very clear and certain, like photographs or satellite maps. But other things, like overheard phone conversations, may have meanings that are difficult to decipher. In order to correctly inter-pret intelligence, agents need to know not just about the sources and references they use, but also the history and significance of the information they've been given.

Delivering

Delivering information means getting it to the right people in a timely manner. Often, reports are needed immediately because an important national decision will be based upon them. Other times, information is collected for later use.

As an example, let's say that the U.S. government is trying to decide whether to move military troops out of Country X. The political situation in Country X has been peaceful. Relations between the United States and Country X have been good for many years. The United States wants to make sure things stay that way, but they also don't want to waste the money and time of the military if they're not needed in Country X. Before any decision is made, the U.S. government wants to be sure there are no threats of future violence.

A U.S. agent assigned to the case would look through newspapers, listen to radio reports (especially

Profile: Alan Turing

Alan Turing (1912–1954) is the founder of computer science as we know it today. His invention, the Turing Machine, a hypothetical mathematical model, reduced information processing to its most basic and simple features. It was designed to imitate human reasoning. Computers today use its concept of input (the question) and output (the answer).

Based on all he had accomplished, Turing was recruited to work with the Government Code and Cypher School during World War II. His training and background helped break the "Enigma" code used by the Germans to send strategy messages within their operation. After the code was broken, the British were able to inter-

cept German messages and use the information against them. Some of the messages came from Adolf Hitler himself. Information decoded by Turing and his colleagues was used to defeat the Germans at Normandy in 1944.

political commentaries), and obtain satellite pictures. Let's say that the agent notices something in one of the photographs and, after further investigation, finds out that it is a training camp for a small terrorist group that wants to take over Country X.

The agent would write his or her report and submit it to the U.S. government, including all the articles, photographs, and interviews that support it. With this information, the U.S. government decides not to risk closing its military base. It also lets Country X know of the potential threat within its own borders.

One of the purposes of this communication is to make the government aware of a potentially serious problem. There is a lot of information out there. Good intelligence-gathering means finding out what needs to be known, like the facts on the development of nuclear or chemical weapons, or plans for terrorist attacks.

Types of Intelligence

The information that secret agents are asked to find falls into three categories. A piece of information may fit into more than one category.

A tactical intelligence officer uses the Images-Many-On-Many computer to assess radar threats during Operation Desert Storm in 1991.

Strategic Intelligence

Strategic intelligence is also called national intelligence. It is the broadest area of information because it concerns both the capabilities and the intentions of a foreign country. Capabilities might be the strength of the country's military, its economic condition, and the general political situation there. But strategic intelligence also takes into account the plans and goals of a country—something that is never known for certain.

Tactical Intelligence

Tactical intelligence is the kind of information military commanders need; it gives them details about a foreign power's armed forces. These days, strategic and tactical intelligence are often very similar. Advances in technology, like satellite maps and computer programs, have changed the way wars are fought and policy is made. Often a military leader will need the same materials as a political leader because technology has blurred the line between political and military concerns.

Counterintelligence

Counterintelligence is the area dedicated to protecting our own country's information. It is also what we use to keep our own intelligence activities secret from others. Successful counterintelligence finds out what other countries are trying to learn about the United States and then finds better ways to keep our secrets. We also use it to fight terrorism and drug trafficking, and to keep our technology safe.

As the director of the Department of Defense Computer Forensics Laboratory, David Ferguson is an important player in counterintelligence investigations.

After all, it's not as if other countries are broadcasting their secrets. Their military strength, political intentions, and role in terrorism are all kept under tight wraps, which is why the agent's job of collecting and interpreting information is so important and challenging. Most of the agent's work is done in an office, reading newspapers and listening to radio broadcasts from the country under investigation. Intelligence work is a lot like writing a research paper. You find as many sources of information as possible, figure out what it all means, and then write a report on it.

The more dramatic intelligence work is obtained from covert sources. This includes getting aerial and satellite pictures, breaking security codes, eavesdropping on important phone conversations, and posing as an ordinary citizen of the country being spied on.

So You Want to Be a Spy

Some people become members of the intelligence community because they decide that's how they want to serve their country. Others are recruited, or asked, to spy.

There is so much information changing hands these days that you might be surprised what is known about you, your family, and your city or town. The IC is always looking for smart and talented people to work for them, especially people who are experts in a particular field (like chemistry or geology) or who know the language, history, and customs of a particular culture.

When someone has the knowledge and ability that an intelligence agency wants, he or she will often be recruited. This means that the agency will ask him or her to spy. You may not think you're spy material, but if you're an expert in chemical engineering who is fluent in eastern European languages, then an intelligence agency may have a job for you.

Generally, double agents are recruited. Sometimes, they are already employed by an intelligence agency. Other times, they are simply the ones who have access to information that another country wants. The story of Kim Philby, Anthony Blunt, Guy Burgess, and Donald Maclean is just one example of how intelligence communities find the agents they need.

The IC is also interested in volunteers. This doesn't mean that the agents won't get paid for their work, or that they'll be automatically accepted by an agency. Instead of being recruited, they'll seek out the agency they want to work for. Some people seek work as agents because they believe that their backgrounds and education offer something valuable to the intelligence community. Perhaps they've lived all over the world and have extensive knowledge of many cultures. Some people volunteer to be agents for the same reason others volunteer to serve in the armed forces—they feel that's the way they can best serve their country.

Profile: Morris "Moe" Berg

Morris "Moe" Berg (1902–1972) is an example of how someone with a variety of talents can be an asset to the U.S. government.

Born in 1902 in New York City, Moe Berg studied languages at Princeton University, played catcher for the Brooklyn Dodgers, and worked as a lawyer.

Berg's intelligence career began when he moved to Washington, DC, where he was often invited to embassy dinners and parties. In 1934, when he was scheduled to tour Japan with an American all-star team, the U.S. government asked him to film Tokyo Harbor and some of the Japanese military bases.

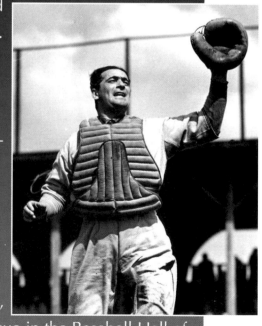

From 1934 until 1941, Berg continued his baseball career while working as a secret agent. He completed a number of missions—including parachuting into Yugoslavia—before joining the staff of the North Atlantic Treaty Organization (NATO) Advisory Group for Aeronautical Research and Development.

Baseball never forgot him, though, and he has been honored with a plaque in the Baseball Hall of Fame in Cooperstown, NY.

Not everyone is so patriotic when it comes to a career. Sometimes, people apply for jobs in the IC simply because they want to do something interesting. The IC offers great benefits for its employees as well as an opportunity to work in an extremely select field.

The CIA doesn't call its people "agents." They are referred to as "clandestine service operations officers." The CIA posts jobs and their requirements on its Web site all the time. Almost all of the posts require a four-year college degree. Besides jobs for engineers, scientists, and secretaries, they are also looking for people with Internet technology skills.

Getting the Job

It's not easy to get a job with an intelligence agency. The application process for most intelligence jobs is extensive. Not only do agencies look for specific skills and abilities, but they also do a broad background check. This means that they'll find out everything you've been doing for the past few years, possibly your whole life.

A hopeful applicant undergoes a lie-detector test to join the Secret Service.

You may also have to take a polygraph, or lie detector, test. Any intelligence agency wants to make sure that the people they hire are honest and trustworthy. After all, a lot is at stake with these jobs.

They'll also ask about your drug history and give you a drug test. If you lie about your past drug use, you can forget about a job with an agency. You can bet they'll find out the truth one way or another. They also have strict guidelines for what is an "acceptable" amount of drug experimentation.

While they understand that sometimes people try drugs just to see what they're like, intelligence agencies are very strict about excessive use. If a person has smoked marijuana more than fifteen times in his or her life—or has smoked it within three years of applying for the job—he or she will not be hired.

If you make it through all of these steps, then you'll generally be put into a training program. However, you could wait up to two years before finding out if you can actually become an agent. Most agencies have probation periods, which they use to see if you're right for the position. During this period, you might work in an office to get used to the procedures of the job. You won't be given any highly classified material, but you'll get to learn a lot about being an agent.

Training

There are ways to find out if you're really interested in the work of a secret agent before going through the application process. Besides doing research, you can also get firsthand experience. Most agencies offer internships to college students. This means that while you're in college, you can also work for an intelligence agency. Many internships take place over the summer. Others let you work while going to school.

If you're interested in being an agent, you should also consider studying a related field in college. Studying languages, criminology (the science of crime and justice), and political science can help your application process. You should also demonstrate a strong interest in foreign affairs. Some high schools have model United Nations, which give kids a chance to see what working for the United Nations is like. You might also travel in order to study the history and language of another country. Many universities offer semester-abroad programs, where you live and attend school in a foreign country.

It's not called the "intelligence" community for nothing. Besides referring to the information it gathers, intelligence is also a quality that its employees must possess. Students should have at least a 3.0 grade-point average (that's a B or better) and a good overall academic record. That means not missing classes, forming good relationships with your teachers, and being involved in extracurricular activities, such as sports or after-school clubs.

Although many agents spend a great deal of time behind their desks, physical fitness is also prized by intelligence agencies. The special training that candidates must undergo often includes a lot of physical conditioning and testing. If you're out in the field, you may need to be able to quickly escape a dangerous situation. And there's not always a taxi available when you want one.

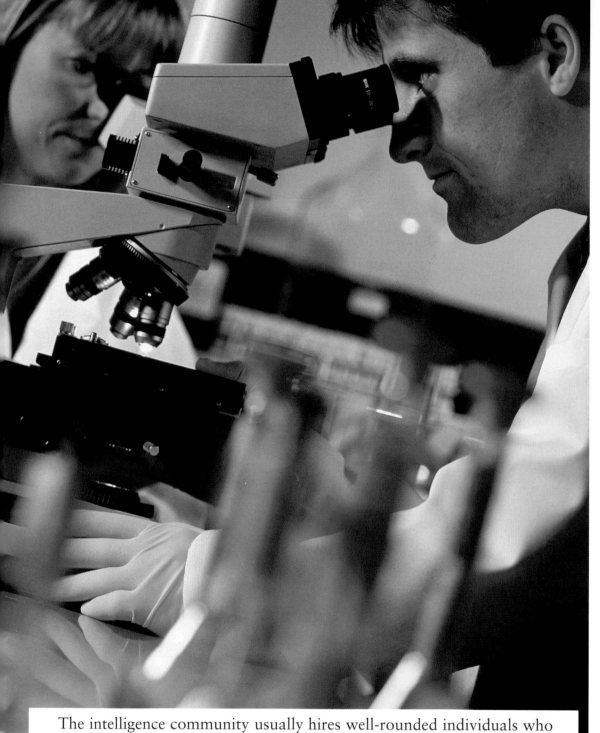

The intelligence community usually hires well-rounded individuals who have demonstrated commitment to a specific field or area of interest.

You don't need to be a track star or a superscholar. The intelligence community just wants people who are well rounded. They are looking for people who have a variety of skills, life experiences, and interests. They also want individuals who have demonstrated commitment, whether it was to a course of study, a job, or a community activity.

Agent Academy

FBI agents spend four months in special training at their academy in Quantico, Virginia. All agents are trained to use deadly force (meaning that they know how to kill someone) and to use a gun, since they carry one at all times. Secret Service agents undergo eight weeks of general investigative training at the Federal Law Enforcement Training Center in Georgia. Afterward, there are nine more weeks of special agent training. The CIA puts agents in different specialized training programs. Each position, from the initial job as a desk officer to the more advanced overseas clandestine operations officer, has its own training program.

New FBI agents participate in a training session at their academy in Quantico, Virginia.

Fantasy Camps

What if you've now decided that, while being a secret agent seemed pretty cool, you're not sure you want to commit your life to it? Lucky for you, there are fantasy and adventure camps that give you the thrill of being a secret agent without the real danger.

These camps assign you a mission, then train you to complete it. Training may include self-defense techniques, espionage skills, high-speed driving instruction, and more. You might be given firearm training (using paintballs instead of real ammunition). Some camps have more extensive programs that last for a week or more and feature actual in-air dog-fights. In all of these camps, the participants leave their real lives behind and behave as though they were real secret agents.

You now know that being a secret agent isn't just breaking into safes and stealing state secrets, but it's not a regular day job either. Secret agents are smart people who come from all walks of life and bring a variety of skills to the job. They can be scientists, economists, mathematicians, or even baseball players and lawyers.

Working as a secret agent requires strong commitment and a great deal of honesty and dedication. You have the choice to make it a rewarding career, a weekend's worth of fun, or just a fantasy in your head. It's up to you, but remember, it's not for the faint of heart!

…Alex drops to the floor and rolls behind the foreign defense minister's desk. The footsteps are

Profile: Aldrich Ames

With the Cold War a fading memory, America was shocked to learn about Aldrich Ames's arrest on February 21, 1994. Who was Ames? No one knew, but his admission that, as a CIA employee, he had been providing the Soviets with classified information for almost a decade made everyone take notice.

According to his confession, Ames had accepted payments from the Soviets that totaled well over $2 million. He had purchased a new Jaguar and an expensive house—in cash—with the funds. No one at the CIA ever suspected Ames of any illegal activities, even though they must have wondered how he could live such a lifestyle on a CIA salary.

It was also discovered that Ames had identified many U.S. spies to the Soviets, which led to their arrests and executions. He was also responsible for feeding incorrect information about the Soviet Union to the U.S. government.

For his relations with Russia, Ames will spend the rest of his life in prison. His wife, Rosario, was sentenced to five years. The CIA is still wondering how such a thing could have gone undetected.

*coming closer. He realizes that he might be dis-
covered, and he reaches for the gun strapped to
his leg.*

*Just then, he hears Leonora's voice from the
hallway: "I'm sorry, but I seem to be lost. Could
you direct me to the ladies' room?"*

*The footsteps move toward the hallway. The
door shuts behind them. Leonora has saved him
once again!*

*Alex opens the safe and finds the codes. He
photographs them with his pen camera, replaces
them, and heads toward the window. Rappelling
down the side of the mansion, he sees Leonora
waiting with the car. It comforts him to know
that within five hours the warhead will be
defused and the country will be safe again.
Mission accomplished.*

Glossary

allegiance   Loyalty.

anonymous   Unknown.

clandestine   Kept secret.

classified   Not for public knowledge, for reasons of national security.

counterespionage   Spying that is used to discover and stop enemy spying.

counterintelligence   Keeping valuable information from an enemy.

covert   Secret.

espionage   The act of using spies to obtain secret intelligence.

ideology   Beliefs

intelligence   Information about an enemy.

probation   A testing period.

recruit   To hire.

rival Competitor.

strategic Relating to military planning and conduct.

tactical Using specific techniques as a way to get a desired outcome.

terrorism Regular use of violence, terror, and intimidation.

treason Betraying your country

For More Information

Central Intelligence Agency (CIA)
Office of Public Affairs
Washington, DC 20505
(703) 482-0623
Web site: http://www.cia.gov
kids' Web site:
http://www.cia.gov/cia/ciakids/index.html

Federal Bureau of Investigation (FBI)
J. Edgar Hoover Building
935 Pennsylvania Avenue NW
Washington, DC 20535-0001
(202) 324-3000
Web site: http://www.fbi.gov

United States Secret Service
Office of Government Liaison and Public Affairs
950 H Street NW
Suite 8400
Washington, DC 20001
(202) 406-5708
Web site: http://www.treas.gov/usss

In Canada

Canadian Security Intelligence Service
P.O. Box 9732
Postal Station T
Ottawa, ON K1G 4G4
(613) 993-9620
Web site: http://www.csis-scrs.gc.ca

James Bond Web Sites

http://www.ianfleming.org
http://www.jamesbond.com

Fantasy Camps

Incredible Adventures
6604 Midnight Pass Road
Sarasota, FL 34242
(800) 644-7382
(941) 346-2603
e-mail: info@incredible_adventures.com
Web site: http://www.covertops.com

Pali Adventures in Southern California
12924 San Vicente Boulevard
Los Angeles, CA 90049
(888) 6-SUMMER (678-6637)
e-mail: info@paliadventures.com
Web site: http://www.paliadventures.com/
    html/pgms/spy.html

For Further Reading

Andryszewski, Tricia. *The Amazing Life of Moe Berg: Catcher, Scholar, Spy.* Brookfield, CT: Millbrook Press, 1996.

Cowen, Ida, and Irene Gunther. *A Spy for Freedom: The Story of Sarah Aaronsohn.* New York: Lodestar Books, 1984.

Factbook on Intelligence. Washington, DC: Central Intelligence Agency, 1997.

Intelligence in the War for Independence. Washington, DC: Central Intelligence Agency, 1997.

Mahoney, M.H. *Women in Espionage: A Biographical Dictionary.* Santa Barbara, CA: ABC-CLIO, 1993.

Martini, Teri. *The Secret Is Out: True Spy Stories.* Boston, MA: Little, Brown, 1990.

Secret Agents: Life as a Professional Spy

O'Toole, G. J. A. *The Encyclopedia of American Intelligence and Espionage.* New York: Facts on File, 1988.

Probert, Ian. *Internet Spy.* New York: Kingfisher, 1996.

Wiese, Jim. *Spy Science: 40 Secret-Sleuthing, Code-Cracking, Spy-Catching Activities for Kids.* New York: Wiley, 1996.

Index

About the Author

Claudia B. Manley is a freelance writer who lives in Brooklyn, New York, with her partner, their son, and their cat.

Photo Credits

Cover © Bill Varie/Corbis; pp. 6, 20, 36 © Corbis; pp. 10, 13 © The Everett Collection; pp. 12, 15, 16, 22, 24, 29, 38, 42, 50, 52 © AP/Wide World Photo; p. 26 © AP/Keystone; p. 34 © AP/BBC; p. 44 © Anna Clopet/Corbis; p. 48 © FPG.

Design and Layout

Les Kanturek